The Quiet One

Tiffany N Thompson

BookLeaf Publishing

India | USA | UK

Presentation by *BookLeaf Publishing*

Web: www.bookleafpub.com

E-mail: info@bookleafpub.com

ISBN: 9789360948856

First edition 2024

ACKNOWLEDGEMENT

I want to thank my Mother who has always inspired me and encouraged me to write.

PREFACE

As far as I can remember, I have been called The Quiet One. It used to annoy me, but now I accept the title. This book of poetry includes some of my innermost thoughts, feelings and experiences. I like to think that I have a vivid imagination and so I also included poems that explored that as well. I am a very private person and this is definitely stepping out of my comfort zone. I made a promise to myself that I would do things a little different this year. I hope you enjoy.

Soft Soft Winds

You left me with no fate
Even though I couldn't stand the hate
You left me with no goodbye
Now you're gone and I still cry
I loved you so
Even though I never let you know
I can still hear the cries and see the pain in his
eyes
Oh those soft...soft... soft...winds

All you wanted was to be brave
Now you're laying in a grave
In this soft fallen ditch
With his your cries I still hear you pitch
I was there when he came
Tears in his eyes
With no one to blame
...Soft...soft.. winds
Blowing in the night

But you didn't give up
Without a fight
You tried so hard to stay on this earth
but failed
Now you're on heavens turf

I wish you would have gotten out of there
And listened to him with his convincing glare
Though you died under the gun
With my praying
You will rise with the sun

...Soft...soft...winds
They will always blow
...Soft...soft...winds
With our help they will grow

...Soft..soft..winds
That's when life begins
If you're smart
You won't let it end
Oh those soft...soft...winds
There's no one else to blame
You can't hide behind the shame
Oh those...young...young...winds
All they wanted was to live
But nothing in return was there to give

Now you're gone

But I still hear your voice
And with these words
I have no choice
Oh those soft...soft...winds...
I hate to say goodbye
Even with tears in my eyes
Goodbye, goodbye goodbye, my friend
Forever you will be my Soft...soft… wind

Blessing

When the noise calms down and the silence
becomes too loud
When the wind stands still and your mind begins
to fill
With a longing for just one more moment
Understand that she was chosen
To take on the role as our Guardian Angel
To protect us
To guide us
When we aren't able
Trust that Love doesn't vanish
When a person is no longer present
It's been branded in our hearts
It's a true blessing

I am

I am a woman
I am a daughter
I am a mother
I am a sister
I am a friend
A colleague
I've been let down
I've been lifted up
I've felt invisible
Overwhelmed
Silenced
Desired
Insecure
Exhausted
Loved
I am funny

I am sarcastic
I am worthy

Love

When I tasted your lips
The feeling was new to me
Like a strange fruit
Now I know the meaning of ecstacy
The way you caressed my soul
Let me know that you wanted more
More than the pleasures of the flesh
Much more than happiness
I knew that you wanted to see beneath my skin
Beyond my heart
I knew that this was more than a physical
attraction
I knew that we didn't need pet names or rings to
bind us together
Or cards to say that we care
For our eyes would say
Kiss me

Hold me
Speak the melodic words that bring me to tears
Give me an invitation into forever
and
I will bring trust, honesty and loyalty
Take my hand in yours and let me lead you to
eternal satisfaction
and
this my love is all that I'm asking

Angel

An Angel appeared to me one day
Distant and with broken wings
Instantly something appealed to me about this
creature
I felt compelled to speak to it

Maybe it was the way it appeared
As if it were lost
Or
Maybe it reminded me of myself
I could tell
That it to had thought it found heaven, but
quickly fell to earth

And the more I spoke with it
I could tell there was a deep connection between
the two of us

And in just a short while of us meeting
This angel
Erased all my worries
Replaced all my fears with expectations
Stole my heart
Ignited my soul
Brightened my days

Heated my nights
And showed me the meaning of love
That angel is you

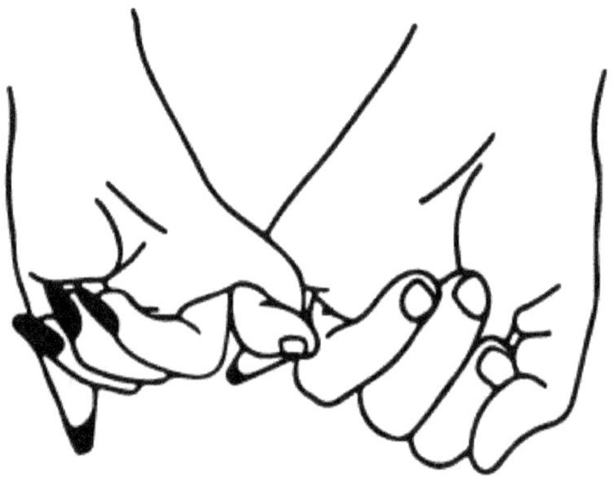

Bill Collectors

You pounce on my back
When I am vulnerable
You scratch
You claw
Try to reveal my entrails
I am defenseless
I can't speak
I'm forced to let go
I now have to pay you attention
Since you've forced me into submission
I am totally inhibited
Oh those damn bill collectors.....

Heaven

It's where aqua green waterfalls
Cascade down into an endless ocean
Where white clouds serve as beds
For all the precious angels
It's where one can eat chocolate covered
almonds and buttermilk pancakes without
feeling guilty
It's where only tears of happiness fall
Where those who were too good for earth
Dwell in the afterlife
Where trumpets blare at the latest arrival
It's where I hope to someday find eternal peace

He is the reason

There is a man in my life
That seems to make what is wrong
Turn out right
I talk to him each and every day
Though little he has to say
He communicates through actions
The slightest problem
He's able to tackle
I love this man for who he is
Because he has been there
During the hardest of years

He is the reason
Why I have hope
He is the reason
With problems I can cope
Though I can't see him
I know that he is there
When I'm down
He helps me bare
For he is the reason
I can go on
He is the epitome of a love so strong

Each day I am so thankful

He is in my life
He loves me completely
In spite
Of my imperfections
To have him in my life is a true blessing
He made me into who I am
I am forever grateful for this man

Paradise

Whether it's
Crystal blue ocean waters
Sand between my toes
Sun glistening against my skin
The wind blowing a slight breeze
or
Having no regrets
Bills paid
Refrigerator full
House filled with love
Laughter encompassing the air
No drama for miles
Supportive family and friends
This is what comes to mind when I think of
Paradise

Hate

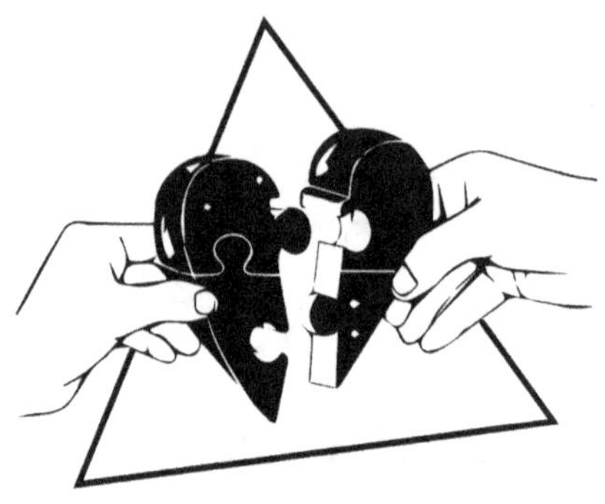

Hate is like a tornado tearing through a town
Uncertain of what will stay on the ground
Scared of the final outcome
Will it be death or eternal damnation
Hate can turn the nicest man cold
Clenching his heart
Strangling his soul
Hate is the opposite of love
It's like a sharp knife
Like a one hundred dollar bill submerged in mud

Hate is one of the strongest emotions
One can become blinded by it
Engulfed in the moment
Hate takes a great amount of energy
It's like the sly grin or phony handshake between
enemies

Hate will fester and grow
Before you know it, it will take over the show
Hate is something not worth giving into
Because love will always shine through

Memories

The smell of cinnamon fills the air
As I measure the ingredients my heart warms
For I can't wait to taste heaven on my lips
I mix
I stir
I sample and I am elated
This is what it used to feel like
When grandma was here
Oh the aroma takes me back to a familiar time
A time of innocence and dependence
I add more sugar to get it just right
Company will be here any minute
And I want them to get a taste of heaven
Even if it's only a spoon full

Eyes

Whether they are brown, blue or green
Affectionate or mean
The eyes never lie
and
That's no surprise

The eyes speak even when you don't utter a
word
With just a glance
They can surely be heard

The eyes can reveal anger, pain and joy
They can can also display an emotional void
The eyes can encompass your inner most
thoughts

The ones that you don't want to share
When you're feeling quite lost
The eyes are the windows to your soul
And within them a story can be told

Nemesis

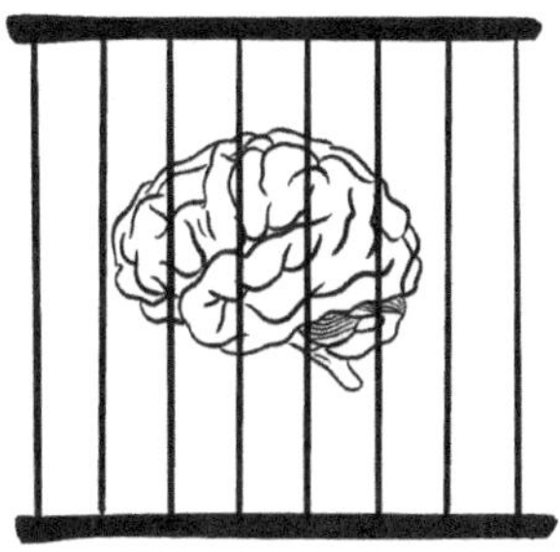

You haunt me at the most inopportune times
When I recognize your presence
Everything seems to stand still
At times I can keep you at bay
Other times
You grab a hold of me and I can't control the
outcome
You overwhelm me
You stifle me
You make me feel awkward
I try to avoid you at all costs
Although not invited
You find a way to keep invading my space
You whisper in my ear
You can't
You won't

You're not good enough
You don't belong in this room
With these people
I know who you truly are
and
I will continue to battle you until you get the
point and never return

Just Be

Be beautiful on the inside and out
Be bold even when filled with doubt
Be brave even when your back is against the
wall
Hold your head high and remember to stand tall
Be aware that she is watching your every move
Be a positive example and
Remember to keep pushing through

X-ray Vision

Superman had it
Even though he is a fictional character
Mothers seem to have it
They can detect a child making a face behind
their back
Now I think I may have the superpower
Right now
You look transparent to me
I can see your adrenaline working overtime
I hear your heart pumping faster than normal
Sweat is glistening from your forehead
Your mouth is dry
You look pale
It's official
You are lying

Daydreaming

I see your face in my dreams
The only thing is
I'm not asleep

I hear your voice
Whisper in my ear
When I go to turn around
You're no longer there

I feel your hand caress my cheek
In a moment's time
You've escaped from me

Full Transparency

The other day you found new ways to please me
I found myself forgiving your past and future
mistakes
Letting the feelings of delusion and
apprehension fade way
I jumped head first into this sea of ecstacy
My rose colored glasses got the best of me
I want to believe that you are a changed human
My heart says, give one more fuck
My mind is in survival mode
The question is, who do I surrender to?

The letter

What would the letter on your chest stand for?
Are you a liar
A cheater
A thief
Or
Does your letter stand for Perfect?
As many think that they are
Make sure that you're holding your own stone
Before you throw it at someone else's glass door

OP

Different location
Same scenarios
Should you speak up or go with the flow?
Does your experience and drive hold its weight?
Seems like the same cast of characters are in place
Make sure you're doing all that's required and more
Fingers crossed
It will get noticed and unlock even greater doors
Don't forget to smile
Always have a positive attitude, but don't be naive
Try not to take things too personal
Don't wear your heart on your sleeve
Never let them see you sweat

Remember you have goals to achieve
So many rules to remember
How can you keep up?
Make sure you do your absolute best
Be approachable and the right amount of tough
How do you really climb that ladder?
Seems to be the million dollar question
Just be careful who you confide in
Don't want to learn that type of hard lesson

B.S.R.

Your beauty is intoxicating
It rarely goes unnoticed
You walk with boundless confidence
Keeping men and women on their toes
Those that have not been personally invited into
your orbit
May view you as arrogant
Your sharp wit is top tier
Your allure is palpable
It can be overwhelming to some
You always hold your head high
Keeping in place
Your invisible crown
You smile at the world as if you know
everyone's inner most thoughts
To the naked eye
You seem to have no imperfections
You appear to have no fear of the unknown
You square up when obstacles invade your space
Overcoming them effortlessly
Not leaving a trace
I sometimes wonder when you get a moment to
yourself
If you get to exhale from holding the world on
your shoulders

Do you allow yourself to be vulnerable?
If only for a second
Does that force field around you dissipate?
Do you get to take in the all the greatness
that you've helped create?

www.ingramcontent.com/pod-product-compliance
Lightning Source LLC
Chambersburg PA
CBHW071236140726
47996CB00007B/2634